MY RAMBLINGS
IN THE
Silence

21 Days of Silent Reflection with the Lord

DR. MICHELE R. WELLS

PUBLISHING

MY RAMBLINGS IN THE SILENCE
21 Days of Silent Reflection with the Lord

Copyright ©2021 by Dr. Michele R. Wells

HOV Publishing a division of HOV, LLC.
www.hovpub.com
hopeofvision@gmail.com

Cover Design: Hope of Vision Designs
Editor/Proofread: Amy A. Owens for Clarity Communications

Contact the Author, Dr. Michele R. Wells at:
drmichelerwells@gmail.com

For further information regarding special discounts on bulk purchases, please visit www.hovpub.com

ISBN Paperback: 978-1-942871-91-0
ISBN eBook: 978-1-942871-92-7

10   9   8   7   6   5   4   3   2   1

Printed in the United States of America

Dedication

I am so thankful to my Lord and Savior Jesus Christ. I am overwhelmed by His love! His grace and mercy never fails! I thank Him for the people in my life who continually encourage me and support me as the Lord continues to show me more of my purpose. I dedicate this devotional to my husband and priest of our home, Alvin Wells who loves me and treats me as a gift from the Lord. I dedicate this work to my mother Elizabeth Dixie who prays tirelessly for me and her family. I dedicate this work to my twin sister Pastor Rachele Dixie who has always been there to speak wisdom into my life. I dedicate this work to my Pastors Cameron and Gwin Minter who have pushed me to grow through their commitment to teaching and living out the Word of God. Lastly, I want to thank my colleagues Dr. Theresa Veach and Dr. David Stefan whose encouragement and support have helped me to complete this work.

Thank you so much.
Dr. Michele

MY RAMBLINGS
IN THE
Silence

About the Author

Gerina Dunwich (whose first name is pronounced "Jereena") is a practicing Witch, an ordained minister (Universal Life Church), and a respected spokesperson for the Pagan community. She considers herself to be a lifelong student of the occult arts and is the author of numerous books on the spellcasting arts and the earth-oriented religion of Wicca. Her most popular titles include *Herbal Magick, Exploring Spellcraft, The Wicca Spellbook, Wicca Craft, The Pagan Book of Halloween, Wicca Candle Magick, Everyday Wicca, Candlelight Spells, Wicca Love Spells,* and *Your Magickal Cat.*

Born under the sign of Capricorn with an Aries rising and her moon in Sagittarius, Gerina is also a professional astrologer and Tarot reader whose diverse clientele include a number of Hollywood celebrities and fellow occult authors. She is the founder of the Bast-Wicca tradition, the Pagan Poets Society, and the Wheel of Wisdom School. Gerina is also a poet and a cat-lover. She writes and plays music and has lived in various parts of world, including a 300-year-old Colonial house near Salem, Massachusetts, and a haunted Victorian mansion in upstate New York. Her interests include herbal folklore, mythology, spiritualism, divination, dreamwork, hypnotism, and past-life regression. Gerina currently lives in Southern California with her Gemini soul mate and their feline familiars.

Contents

Foreword

In a world where we experience so much chaos and at times so much unrest, it is vitally important that we take time to rest in silence. In this wonderful work by Dr. Michele R. Wells, we have a chance to focus our thoughts on what silence means. Being able to come back to a word that centers us in the midst of a mind that oftentimes will race without our permission, Dr. Wells shares an opportunity right here for you and me to just be in the presence of a merciful and loving, grace-giving God.

In these moments of Silence, we receive so much more than what we could ever give out. However, if we do not take these moments, we will miss out on what God wants to do in and through our lives. So we are so grateful and blessed that Dr. Wells took this journey and through it God gave her the words to share with us, so that we too have an opportunity to engage with the silence.

My Ramblings in the Silence will comfort you, it will give you pause, it will give you an opportunity to separate from all of the distractions and turbulence that can be around us from day-to-day. In that pause and separation, we have an opportunity to grow and deepen our walk with the Lord. He will show us greater purpose and He will show us greater wisdom as we allow His Spirit to engage us. My Ramblings in the Silence is a "right now work." It is a work that will give each and every one of you the opportunity that you need to walk through your journey and come out on the other side with greater victory.

Thank you, Dr. Michele R. Wells, for allowing the Lord to use you and for your obedience in sharing what I believe is the heart of God for each of us. I believe your heart and I believe I know your heart, so I am so grateful that you have honored each of us with a glimpse into your very soul. Dr. Michele R. Wells, you are a blessing and a light for so many. Thank you for walking out a portion of God's great purpose in you through My Ramblings in the Silence.

Now to each of you, please journey with us as we enter into the Silence. God will indeed meet you there and you will find yourself with a greater perspective on what it means to listen for the voice of God. As you and I listen, we will receive the richness of the Father. God bless you all in this journey.

Pastor Rachele Dixie, MDiv., MA

Introduction

This devotional, My Ramblings in the Silence, is inspired by Thomas Keating's method of Centering Prayer. This practice allows you to sit in the silence and hear the silence. I am a work-in-progress with centering myself. Some days I rest in it and some days I struggle with it. Each day of this devotional I will share what I found in the silence or simply through my time in prayer. There was a shift when I left the work for a season and then returned to it. I was not the same.

I encourage you to sit in silence before you read the day's devotion or have your own time with the Lord and ask Him what He is speaking for you that day. Progressively through the 21 days your time sitting in the silence will increase. There is a word, a sacred word each day, to guide you in the silence. You may find that you want to use a different word and that is okay. This is your journey with God. The sacred word is simply used to redirect your thoughts back to Him and push out the distractions. I invite you to read My Ramblings in the Silence out loud after your time and then journal what God is speaking to you in the silence and/or through your time of prayer.

Some days my ramblings may make more sense than on other days because they are truly my ramblings— what God spoke as I sat in silence, and as prayed and how I processed it. Each day has scripture to meditate upon and/or a prayer. I encourage you to dig deeper into the scriptures that are shared. I invite you into this journey so that you can find the same beauty in the silence that I am finding. Know that it does not have to be some perfect word that comes or some perfect experience that happens. It is an opportunity to "just be" with God. See where it takes you and experience how you can draw closer to Him.

This is the website for more information on Thomas Keating's Centering Prayer if you are interested in exploring Centering Prayer further.

For more information:

https://www.contemplativeoutreach.org/category/category/centering-prayer

Exhortation as you Begin

Go all in! Stop skirting the edges of your relationship with the Father. Are you willing? Are you willing to sit in the silence and hear and obey? Follow the instructions given in the silence. It means putting aside the old way and the *stinking thinking*. It means letting your thoughts and your ways be guided by the Father. Sometimes that is uncomfortable but discomfort is what moves us to change. Temper your words even as you pray and as you speak to those around you. Go all in to the Silence and be changed!

Instructions for the Silence

1. Plan your time for the silence.

2. Get in a quiet place.

3. Remove distractions like the phone, television etc.

4. Choose how long you want to sit in the silence (you may desire to increase your time as you continue the practice).

5. Set a timer.

6. Sit in a comfortable position.

7. Take some deep cleansing breaths.

8. Ask the Lord to give you a sacred word.

9. Begin the timer.

10. As you sit, block everything out of your mind. If you find your mind drifting to other thoughts use the sacred word to gently guide you back to the silence.

11. When the timer goes off slowly open your eyes.

12. Take some deep cleansing breaths.

13. Journal what the Lord is speaking to your spirit.

Day 1: Lord

(I encourage you to read out loud)

Why is it so hard "to be?" Why is it so hard to sit in the silence and let Him be **Lord**? My thoughts drift to things of the day. My heart issues, the ugly things in my heart creep in asking *Who or what is my **Lord**?* Am I so caught up in myself that I cannot let Jesus be **Lord**? How unfortunate for me. My flesh holds nothing good. At best, my heart is unclean, and my thoughts are uncertain. My deepest NEED is to let Jesus be **Lord**!

What does that mean? To let You be **Lord**? To let... to relinquish my control and my right to be in control. You are the sovereign **Lord**, full of grace and truth. Full, nothing lacking. To be...there, present, in the moment; in every moment...**Lord**...over all, sovereign; in control. Forgive me and help me for You are **Lord**! **Lord**...one having power or authority to whom service and obedience are due (merriam-webster.com/dictionary). Ahh, I see it now. I don't want to let go of my power and yet I would have no power at all if it were not for my **Lord**!

> *But you, O LORD, are a shield around me; you are my glory, the one who holds my head high. (Psalm 3:3, NLT)*

> *I said to the LORD, "You are my Master! Every good thing I have comes from you." (Psalm 16:2, NLT)*

> *Then I pray to you, O LORD. I say, "You are my place of refuge. You are all I really want in life. (Psalm 142:5, NLT)*

My Prayer for You

I am reflecting this morning and thinking of all of you. I pray that you are taking time to sit in the silence and center yourselves. To focus on the sacred words that draw you back to Christ. To hear the Holy Spirit as He speaks ever so sweetly to you. I pray that you are blessed in all that you do and that as He draws you closer, that you will fulfill the good purpose that He

has designed for you, using every gifting that He has
revealed and those yet to be revealed for His glory.

Journal question

How do I allow Him to be Lord in my life?

_____

_____

_____

_____

_____

_____

_____

_____

_____

_____

_____

_____

_____

_____

_____

Day 2: Release

I could not hear today. The anxiety overshadowed the silence. The word that the Lord spoke to me was, **release**; but I could not. I gave up the silence and immediately moved to the "to do" list. It is unfortunate, because in anxiety there is no peace; it escapes me. I am rushed into uncertainty, into the fear, into a feeling of inadequacy. I find it difficult to grab hold of my confident hope so that I can eagerly walk into whatever purpose the day holds. I go anyway leaving the silence behind, knowing that it waits for me. I have to choose Him (the silence) because He has already chosen me. But, I rush into the day to see if I belong to whatever it has to offer, but the silence says, "You already do belong!" **RELEASE**

Release my cares and fears to the Father. **Release** my plans and thoughts. Release my pride. Look to Him as my confident hope. Know that the plans that *He* has for my day are so much greater than the plans that I have for my day. Do my plans include Him? Is He the priority in all that I do? **RELEASE** and allow Him to guide and direct my steps.

Prayer

Father, in the name of Jesus, take all of my anxiety, worry, and fear. I release that You. It does not belong to me so I leave it to you because Jesus took care of it on the cross. When I try to take it back I am doubting that you are able. Speak to me, throughout this day, those things that you want me to hear. Use me in ways that honor you. I choose You today fully and completely, in Jesus' name, Amen!

Journal question

How can I release the cares of the day so that I can hear Him in the silence?

_____

_____

_____

_____

Day 3: New

I have spoken that I am in the **new**, but I have not acted on the **new**. The **new** requires something to change. Something different transpires in the **new**. The end result is something that I have never experienced before. The **new** is not easy. Anxiety and distraction await on the journey to the **new**. Fear rears its ugly head, but in the **new** I keep moving through fear. I don't stop until I get to the **new**. How do I know when I am there?

The **new** is perpetual. The **new** is every day that you take a different path or make a different decision at the leading of the Lord; something that I have not or would not have done before. The **new** is refreshing, joyful, peaceful, hopeful; that is the **new**. That is where I am going when I choose to act on it. When I find myself in the same place as before then I have let go of the **new** again. The beautiful thing is that I can pick it up again. Don't stop! The **new** awaits. Eyes haven't seen the **new**, ears haven't heard the new. But the **new** is prepared for those that Love Me. Be **NEW!**

Meditate on Scripture

> *That is what the Scriptures mean when they say, "No eye has seen, no ear has heard, and no mind has imagined what God has prepared for those who love him."*
>
> *(1 Corinthians 2:9, NLT)*
>
> *This means that anyone who belongs to Christ has become a new person. The old life is gone; a new life has begun! (2 Corinthians 5:17, NLT)*

Journal question

What is the new that you are longing to experience, but have been too afraid to pursue? Write a prayer asking the Lord to help you to pursue it.

_____

_____

Day 4: Hear

Sitting in the silence is deafening. I can't **hear** because I'm so focused on my physical body and what I feel. All I **hear** are my thoughts and they are not good. The silence wants to speak, but it is waiting for me to listen. I'm trying but it's a battle! Why is it such a battle? What don't I want to **hear?** The silence is so dark, but it should be light. Why am I on the dark side of the silence? For so long, I have let everything drown out the silence. I've listened to the other voices and ignored the silence. Now I have to fight my way back to the light, so that I can **hear** Him. I will keep fighting to **hear** the silence.

Is it that I can't **hear** because it brings me discomfort? I want to be comfortable and yet even in trying to be comfortable I am not. If I would really **hear** the silence, then my comfort and my peace will come near. Then I could really **hear!**

Meditate on Scripture

"For everything that is hidden will eventually be brought into the open, and every secret will be brought to light. Anyone with ears to hear should listen and understand. (Mark 4:22-23, NLT)

Prayer

Heavenly Father pour your light into my heart today. Give me an ear to know your voice. Let me hear and listen. Bring me comfort in the discomfort so that I can move forward in what you are calling for from me. I will trust your voice and will not allow my thoughts to drown it out. I choose to hear and obey. In Jesus' name, Amen!

Journal question

What prevents you from being able to fully listen in the silence? What are the hidden things that God has revealed to you today?

Day 5: Comfort

Today I found it in the silence, **comfort**. I heard the "I love you" in the silence. It put a smile on my face and gave me such peace. The very thing that I run from, that I fear, is there in the silence; but it is not to be feared. In the silence there is **comfort**. There is a rest in the silence that I still have to fight for, but it is there. Keep coming back to the silence. Many thoughts come in the silence, but there is opposition on the outside of the silence. Inside the silence however, there's an emptying out of all fear, of all worry, of all doubt. Once that is all emptied out, there is rest in peace and **comfort** in the silence. The cares of life do not loom over me when I rest in the **comfort** of the silence.

Meditate on Scripture

> *And I will pray the Father, and he shall give you another Comforter, that he may abide*

*with you forever; Even the Spirit of truth;
whom the world cannot receive, because it
seeth him not, neither knoweth him: but ye
know him; for he dwelleth with you, and
shall be in you. I will not leave you
comfortless: I will come to you. (John 14:
16-18, KJV)*

*The seeds that fell among the thorns
represent those who hear the message, but
all too quickly the message is crowded out
by the cares and riches and pleasures of this
life. And so they never grow into maturity.
(Luke 8:14, NLT)*

Prayer

*Heavenly Father, thank You for not giving up on me.
Thank You for bringing me comfort and peace when I
find You in the silence. Thank You for showing me that
it is worth fighting for to find You. I release the cares
of this life so that I can grow into maturity. Thank You
for making me aware of the opposition. I recognize
that I have to keep pursuing You to find You and when*

I do find You I am reminded by the Comforter that You will never leave me comfortless! I praise and thank You, in Jesus' name, Amen!

<u>Journal question</u>

How are you empowered by the comfort that you find in the silence?

_____

_____

_____

_____

_____

_____

_____

_____

_____

_____

_____

_____

_____

Day 6: Breath

I found my **breath** today in the silence. I found thankfulness in the silence. I found faith in the silence. I found provision in the silence. I found goodness in the silence. I found God in the silence. The enemy tried to bully me out of the silence, but the silence is stronger than him. The more I wait and sit in the silence, the stronger I become. I find my **breath**. My **breath** comes from You. You breathed life into me. Yes, my anxious thoughts are still there. Images that I don't want to see. But, the longer I wait in the silence the more they disappear and I gain my **breath**. The **breath**, the very source of my life, is found in the silence. It is getting better in the silence. It is getting sweeter in the silence. My heart's desire is to want more of the silence.

Meditate on Scripture

*Then the L*ORD *God formed a man from the dust of the ground and breathed into his nostrils the breath of life, and the man became a living being. (Genesis 2:7, NIV)*

The God who made the world and everything in it is the Lord of heaven and earth and does not live in temples built by human hands. And he is not served by human hands, as if he needed anything. Rather, he himself gives everyone life and breath and everything else. (Acts 17:24-25, NIV).

Prayer

Father, in Jesus' name, give me strength to press into the silence. Let me find more of you there. Let me rest in the peace that is there. Give me the strength to fight against the enemy. Consume my thoughts in the silence so much that they will not be able to return during my day. Only thoughts of faith, provision, thankfulness, and goodness will consume me through my day because of my time in the silence. Thank you, Lord for your breath. Amen.

<u>Journal question</u>

After reading this devotion, does the phrase, "I need to catch my breath," have a different meaning to you?

_____

_____

_____

_____

_____

_____

_____

_____

_____

_____

_____

Day 7: Longing

There was contention again today for the silence. The silence came and then it left. Perhaps I should say that I found myself in the silence, but then I lost the battle to stay. In the silence I found these words...*If you seek me you will find me...if you seek me with all of the longing in your heart*. **Longing.** A want. A need. A strong desire. I have to first long for the silence so that I can find Him. There is an emptiness in me without the silence. There is an anxious wanting, but never finding without the silence. This is harder than I thought. I want it, but do I want it enough? I have to want it more. I fight for it, but I am not fighting hard enough. The battle is won in the silence. Interesting. You have to fight for the silence, **long** for the silence in order to win the fight in the silence. I realize I must contend for the silence even more.

Meditate on Scripture

> **Then [with a deep longing] you will seek Me and require Me [as a vital necessity] and [you will] find Me when you search for Me with all your heart. (Jeremiah 29:13, AMP)**

Prayer

Heavenly Father I simply ask today that You would work on my heart. I want to long more for You than I ever have before. I want to long for you more than anything. I realize that I fall short. I rely on Your grace and the new mercies of each day to bring me back to You. Thank you for loving me enough to not give up on me and to change my heart that I might long for You alone. I open my heart and surrender today, in Jesus' name, Amen!

Journal question

What message is today's scripture speaking to you? What is your heart longing for with the Father? Can you find it in the silence? Why or why not?

Day 8: My Soul

I woke up today to a beautiful silence that penetrated my **soul.** A rest. A peace. A joy. A calm. A place where I wanted to be and to stay. Hope is there. Thankfulness is there. I heard the roar of a train coming. Even that made me think of all of creation being His. And then, it slowly faded into the distance and the sweet silence remained. It is always here with me. Today it is tangible. I feel it. It loves me and I love it. I want and desire it to stay. There is nothing sweeter.

Meditate on Scripture

> *Jesus replied, "You must love the Lord your God with all your heart, all your soul, and all your mind." (Matthew 22:37, NLT)*

Mary responded, "Oh, how my soul praises the Lord. How my spirit rejoices in God my Savior! (Luke 1:46-47, NLT)

Oh, that men would give thanks to the LORD for His goodness, And for His wonderful works to the children of men! For He satisfies the longing soul and fills the hungry soul with goodness. (Psalms 107:8-9, NKJV)

Journal question

The soul is our mind, our will, and our emotions. How can surrendering your spirit man in the silence heal your soul? Write a prayer asking for that healing.

_____

_____

_____

_____

_____

_____

_____

Day 9: Seek

When I **seek** Him in the silence, there are so many invasions into the silence. Not necessarily good or bad, they just are. I hear so much more when I am **seeking** Him in the silence. Until now, I have fought so hard <u>not to be there</u> because it causes me to examine myself. Now, the Lord is saying I have to fight even harder <u>to be there</u>. Physical discomfort invades the silence. Cares of this life invade the silence. Busyness invades the silence. I feel like I am wandering right outside the door of the silence periodically finding my way in. I just want to always be able to step in and find the solace of my Savior. However, it will not come without this warring. But, I am sure that it will come if I keep **seeking**. I believe the more I **seek,** the easier it will be to remain in His presence.

Meditate on Scripture

> *Seek the LORD while you can find him. Call on him now while he is near... (Isaiah 55:6, NLT)*

> *"Keep on asking, and you will receive what you ask for. Keep on seeking, and you will find. Keep on knocking, and the door will be opened to you. For everyone who asks, receives. Everyone who seeks, finds. And to everyone who knocks, the door will be opened. (Matthew 7:6-8, NLT)*

Journal question

What does it mean for you to seek the Lord? What are the invasions that keep you from doing so?

_____

_____

_____

_____

_____

Day 10: Quiet

Peace and **quiet** in the silence. **Quiet** my heart. **Quiet**. Stop thinking and musing on the things that are concerning me. The Lord says to **Quiet** myself to hear and meditate on the things that are a concern to Him. I am reminded of the nothingness that came when I fell unconscious one time. My brain was completely quiet. No thoughts, no worries, no plans, just peace. Even in the fight for the silence invasions come. The silence says come back to me. Seek peace and pursue it. That is why peace is tied to **quiet**. There is a quietness of the thoughts. The cares of this life are not invited into the **quiet**. They are dealt with in the **quiet**. They are dealt with by being invaded with peace.

Meditate on Scripture

He calms the storm, So that its waves are still. Then they are glad because they are quiet; So He guides them to their desired haven. (Psalm 107:29-30, NKJV)

LORD, my heart is not proud; my eyes are not haughty. I don't concern myself with matters too great or too awesome for me to grasp. Instead, I have calmed and quieted myself, like a weaned child who no longer cries for its mother's milk. Yes, like a weaned child is my soul within me. (Psalms 131:1-2, NLT)

Journal question

What are these scriptures speaking to you about the quiet? What is your response to the Lord? Write it as a prayer unto Him.

_____

_____

_____

_____

_____

Day 11: Trust

Trust the silence. When I **trust** the silence it wraps me in comfort, rest, and peace. It is a refreshing place. Even when the silence is invaded by the sounds of the world outside, I'm still reminded to **trust**. I may hear cars, trains, or planes overhead, but think of it; each of those will only reach their destination through (blind) **trust**. I **trust** each and every day without even thinking about it. The silence reminded me to be intentional about **trusting**. When my thoughts are invaded with busyness, **trust**. Sometimes I create my own busyness by not **trusting.** Today there was so much **trust** and rest in the silence that I really wanted to stay! Even though thoughts wanted to push me out, **trust** wrapped me up and let me rest in the silence.

Prayer

Father, Your word says in Proverbs 3:5-6, ***"Trust in the LORD with all your heart; do not depend on your*** *own understanding. Seek his will in all you do, and he will show you which path to take."* Father, today I ask you to help me to be intentional about trusting the path that You have set for me. Forgive me for my lack of trust and fill me today with a renewed trust in You; knowing that You are the Sovereign Lord and that You know my end from the beginning. I trust that Your plans for me are good. In all the plans You have set for me I trust that You will be honored and receive the glory! In Jesus' name, Amen!

> **"For I know the plans I have for you," says the LORD. "They are plans for good and not for disaster, to give you a future and a hope." (Jeremiah 29:11, NLT)**

Journal question

What are some of the things that derail your trusting God? How can you be more intentional about trusting Him?

Day 12: Grace

Today I fell into the Silence by His **grace**. I found myself wrapped in the silence and the undeserved love known as **Grace**. Today I have **Grace** for every interaction. Today I'm reminded of the grace of safety, of life, of breath, of love. The rise and fall of my chest as I breathe is because of **Grace**. The place that I sit in the silence resting in it is because of **Grace**. The wave of peace that I feel is because of **Grace**. The opportunity for this new day and all that it holds is because of **Grace**. Today, **Grace** will enable me to handle those things that I am unable to handle in my own strength!

Meditate on Scripture

> *But he answered me, "My grace is always more than enough for you, and my power finds its full expression through your weakness." So I will celebrate my*

weaknesses, for when I'm weak I sense more deeply the mighty power of Christ living in me. (2 Corinthians 12:9, TPT)

<u>Prayer</u>

Most gracious God my Father I thank You today for giving me the grace that is the underserved favor and blessing of You. I am overwhelmed by Your love. Let me extend that same grace and love to others and show Your glory! In Jesus' name, Amen!

<u>Journal question</u>

What is the scripture speaking to you personally about God's grace for your life?

_____

_____

_____

_____

_____

_____

_____

Day 13: Let this Mind Be

Today I heard a phrase as my thoughts were overtaking me in the silence, **"Let this mind be!"** The scripture says in ***Philippians 2:5 "Let this mind be in you that was also in Christ Jesus."*** As I drift in and out of the silence, I meditate on each word. **Let**...choose to take on this mind because there is a mind whose thoughts are dark and harried. **This mind**...is opposite of the mind that meditates on things that are not glorifying the Father. This is the mind that has been given to me by my Heavenly Father. I have to take ownership of it and steward it well. And then, be. **To be**...to rest with this mind; to settle with this mind; to operate with this mind. The silence still was a battle today, but this will walk with me to draw me back when the thoughts take me to places that are overwhelming and draw me away from God's peace and presence. Today I will be drawn back by **letting this mind be in me!**

Meditate on Scripture

And now, dear brothers and sisters, one final thing. Fix your thoughts on what is true, and honorable, and right, and pure, and lovely, and admirable. Think about things that are excellent and worthy of praise. (Philippians 4:8, NLT)

Prayer

Father in the Name of Jesus I want to thank you for the mind that You have given me. I pray that my mind and thoughts are always surrendered to You. I choose today to give You every thought and use the mind that You have given me to glorify You. My thoughts rest in You today. You are my Creator and sustain my life. I have this mind because of Your goodness. I will use this mind to glorify and praise You with my thoughts. I will let the mind that You have given me mirror the mind of my Lord and Savior Jesus Christ. Amen!

<u>Journal question</u>

Think on the mind. How do you draw your thoughts
back to things that are edifying when you are caught
in negative thinking?

_____

_____

_____

_____

_____

_____

_____

_____

_____

_____

_____

_____

_____

_____

Day 14: Time

The silence is beautiful when I spend it with the Father. Even through the tears and the pain there arises a peace and a love that this world can never give. Nothing compares to the weight of My Father's Spirit upon me and in me. No trial that the enemy brings is weightier than His love. His power invades every trial and His light invades every form of darkness. I know and rest in this when I spend **time** in the silence with Him. His Presence in the silence is the strength that I need to walk into every battle and defeat every foe. Focused silence invites His presence. I have to press, I have to want it, I have to seek it. I will find Him if I seek Him with all of My heart. He is there ready to pour out His love upon me. He says, "take **time** with Me and meet me here in the silence."

Meditate on Scripture

You will call to Me and come and pray to Me, and I will listen to you. You will seek Me and find Me when you search for Me with all your heart. (Jeremiah 29:12-13, HCSB)

So God set another time for entering his rest, and that time is today. God announced this through David much later in the words already quoted: "Today when you hear his voice, don't harden your hearts." (Hebrews 4:7, NLT)

Journal question

What distracts you from taking time with the Lord? Do you long for that time with Him or does it seem like a chore? Write your prayer unto Him about spending time in His presence.

_____

_____

Day 15: No Condemnation

God is breaking the cycle of defeat in my life. In the silence I may find mourning and sorrow, but when I come out of the sorrow there is a breakthrough! God is patient, loving, and kind and His word declares that there is **no condemnation** to them that are in Christ (Romans 12:1). Condemnation comes from the enemy not from God. If I am condemned, it is because I have allowed lies and sin to reign in my body and mind. I have given authority of my thoughts and actions to the enemy.

> *So you also should consider yourselves to be dead to the power of sin and alive to God through Christ Jesus. Do not let sin control the way you live; do not give in to sinful desires. (Romans 6:11-12, NLT)*

BUT there is victory! The victory is that God is a forgiving God. It is simple. In the silence use the sorrow, to repent, and to receive forgiveness and move forward in the Lord. Let your season of silence draw you close to the Lord and **away from condemnation.** You are not defeated, you are victorious!

Meditate on Scripture

> *You were dead because of your sins and because your sinful nature was not yet cut away. Then God made you alive with Christ, for He forgave all our sins. He canceled the record of the charges against us and took it away by nailing it to the cross. (Colossians 2:13-14, NLT)*

Prayer

Heavenly Father, your word reminds us in Romans 12:1 that there is no condemnation to them that are in Christ Jesus. Help me to find myself in You. Help me to surrender my life, my thoughts, my ways to the victory that comes through You. Grant me Your peace and healing that I might let go of anything that would keep me in a place of condemnation. I declare my freedom today and thank you for my life being hidden in Christ Jesus. I declare that I walk in the Spirit of the Lord and not in my flesh. Thank You for the promise that comes when I walk fully in You, in Jesus' name, Amen!

Journal question

As you reflect, have you been caught in the spirit of condemnation? How will you use your time in the silence to break free of this spirit?

_____

_____

_____

_____

_____

_____

_____

_____

_____

_____

Day 16: Victory

In the silence conviction comes. Don't ignore it. The deep wounds and pains that have kept me bound to strongholds are revealed in the silence. The way through is revealed in the silence. Freedom is revealed in the silence. The way through, the freedom that I seek requires obedience to letting go of old ways. Rely on His grace in these times. As Paul was plagued with a "thorn" he needed and relied on the grace of God (*2 Corinthians 12:9*). I cannot do it in my strength. Failure is inevitable, but it is not the end. God has healing for me. He has **victory** for me! I sit at the right hand along with Jesus and hence the **victory** is already won!

> **Ephesians 2:4-6 says, "*But God is so rich in mercy, and he loved us so much, that even though we were dead because of our sins, He gave us life when He raised Christ from the dead. (It is only by God's grace***

that you have been saved!) For He raised us from the dead along with Christ and seated us with him in the heavenly realms because we are united with Christ Jesus." (NLT)

Although **victory** comes with a battle and there is a cost for the win, I can be at peace knowing that is mine! If I would just take the step and surrender the things to God that keep me bound each day, I know that I will look back and see the victory.

"Let me be clear, the Anointed One has set us free—not partially, but completely and wonderfully free! We must always cherish this truth and stubbornly refuse to go back into the bondage of our past." (Galatians 5:1, TPT)

When I am walking and getting tired, heading for home, I look back and see how far I have come. Those steps have already been taken! Every step represents **victory** and those victories have been won!

Prayer

Father, in the name of Jesus, I thank You for the victory that I have through Jesus Christ. I no longer want to be bound to anything that this world has to offer, but I want to receive the complete freedom given to me through the sacrifice of Jesus Christ. I thank You for revealing the strongholds that need to be torn down in my life. I set them loose and as I let them go I cling to You, in Jesus' name, Amen!

Journal question

What strongholds has God revealed to you that need to be broken in your life? Write your own prayer of release from those strongholds.

_____

_____

_____

_____

_____

_____

Day 17: Control

In the silence I realize when I am in the grip of fear. Sometimes I can be so strong and courageous. I can pray prayers that I know will bring a breakthrough. Then come the days when confusion and doubts seem to abound. I am reading the word and I am praying but I am still wavering between two options; with— trusting God or listening to the enemy. Yes, I have options. That is the beauty of who God is. He gives me choices. He is not a controlling God, but I can allow Him to be in control of my life and order my steps. When I give God **control**, although sometimes it can be painful, God is pruning me so that I will bear more fruit in my life.

> *John 15:1-2 says, "I am the true grapevine, and my Father is the gardener. He cuts off every branch of mine that doesn't produce fruit, and he prunes the branches that do*

bear fruit so they will produce even

more. (NLT)

See, when things do not turn out my way, if they seem too hard to handle, or if it hurts too much, then I want to take **control** back because I don't want it to be hard. I don't want to be pruned. I let fear come in and overtake my trust in God. But, if I really, REALLY give it to God, I can rest because He is doing it for my good so that my life will bear fruit. Do I want to rest in God? I have noticed that I have to fight for it. Yes, I fight for rest! But, once I have really, REALLY given up the **control** there is peace; unexplainable peace and fruitfulness in my life.

Meditate on Scripture

So there is a special rest still waiting for the

people of God. For all who have entered

into God's rest have rested from their

labors, just as God did after creating the

world. So let us do our best to enter that

rest. But if we disobey God, as the people of

Israel did, we will fall. (Hebrews 4: 9-11, NLT)

Journal question

Can you identify times when you have taken back the control instead of allowing God to lead? What was the outcome?

_____

_____

_____

_____

_____

_____

_____

_____

_____

_____

_____

_____

_____

Day 18: Cooperate

Father God is gracious! He has amazing plans for me. He wants me to **cooperate** with His plans for my life and not the other way around. He says be healed. Stop bringing up the traumas of your past and be healed. **Cooperate** with My healing. If I want a peaceful mind I must **cooperate** with scriptures of peace.

> *Don't be pulled in different directions or worried about a thing. Be saturated in prayer throughout each day, offering your faith-filled requests before God with overflowing gratitude. Tell him every detail of your life, then God's wonderful peace that transcends human understanding, will make the answers known to you through Jesus Christ. (Philippians 4:6-7 TPT)*

If I want a healed body I have to **cooperate** with physical health.

All athletes are disciplined in their training. They do it to win a prize that will fade away, but we do it for an eternal prize. So I run with purpose in every step. I am not just shadowboxing. I discipline my body like an athlete, training it to do what it should. Otherwise, I fear that after preaching to others I myself might be disqualified. (I Corinthians 9:25-27, NLT)

If I want healed emotions I have to **cooperate** with reading, studying, and praying His word over my life situations. If I want a strong marriage, I have to **cooperate** with Him in communication with my spouse. He says, turn to Me in times of sorrow. Look to Me for your hope. Look to Me for your healing. **Cooperate** with Me! The scripture in **1 Peter 2:24** is not just about physical healing but God's healing in every area of my life.

"He himself carried our sins in his body on the cross so that we would be dead to sin and

live for righteousness. Our instant healing flowed from his wounding." (TPT)

<u>Prayer</u>

Heavenly Father I ask you today to help me to cooperate with You and focus my mind on Your total sufficiency. I receive the healing that you want to bring to every hurt and trauma that I have faced. I receive the healing in my physical body that Christ won on the cross. I ask for a spirit of discipline for my mind, body, and my Spirit man. Let me cooperate with You that I might be made fully whole, in Jesus' name, Amen!

<u>Journal</u>

Write down the areas in your life where you need to experience the Lord's healing. Write a prayer that you can pray specifically for healing in that area.

_____

_____

_____

Day 19: Conviction

In the silence great **conviction** comes upon me and I realize that I am so connected to this world. When I know what is right to do, yet I continue to fight against it, that means that I have allowed the things of this world to become my idol. God said, ***"You shall have no other gods before me." (Exodus 20:3)*** Whatever I put before Him has become my god. The gods of this world bring pleasure, but they also grip me with fear. Fear, because I know that I have dishonored the one true God, my God, my Lord and resurrected, Savior Jesus Christ. Fear because the gods of this world only lead to destruction. I thank God that He gives correction to those whom He loves. ***Proverbs 3:11-13 says, "My child, when the Lord God speaks to you, never take his words lightly, and never be upset when he corrects you. For the Father's discipline comes only from his passionate love and pleasure for you. Even when it seems like his correction is harsh,*** *it's still better than any father on earth gives to his child." (TPT)*

Thank God that He loves me with a passionate love. I welcome the **conviction** that comes upon my heart so that I can be drawn back to my Father. Because of this I have a hope and it is victory through Christ Jesus!

Meditate on Scripture

> *"Yet even in the midst of all these things, we triumph over them all, for God has made us to be more than conquerors, and his demonstrated love is our glorious victory over everything!" (Romans 8:37, TPT)*

Journal

Identify the things in your life that you have allowed to become idols. What will you do when you sense that you are giving more glory to the idols than you are to God? Write a prayer about what God is revealing to you.

Day 20: It

In the silence **"it"** keeps coming. What is **"it"**? That nagging and tugging at my heart that God wants more from me. As much as I want **"it"** to be settled, **it** keeps bringing me before the Lord. **It** keeps requiring me to seek more, to pray more, to fast more! As I consider a limitless God, I am bound by the limits of my mind and my experience. To move into the supernatural there has to be a relinquishing of my soul—my mind, my will, my emotions—and my limits. I have found myself clothing my pride in humility, but I am not fooling Him. God is showing me that I need to be aware to not allow the spirit of pride back in. The word of God tells me that He can do more than I can think or imagine. If I would give **"it"** (pride, envy, jealousy, inadequacy) to Him it will be beyond my wildest thoughts and dreams. **"It"** keeps me truly humble and reminds me that I am nothing without my limitless God.

Meditate on Scripture

"Never doubt God's mighty power to work in you and accomplish all this. He will achieve infinitely more than your greatest request, your most unbelievable dream, and exceed your wildest imagination! He will outdo them all, for his miraculous power constantly energizes you." (Ephesians 3:20, TPT)

Prayer

Father God I want to offer you praise! You are limitless! There is nothing that is too hard for You! I pray today that I will stop holding You back and that I will allow You to saturate every area of my life. I repent for my pride and my limited ways of thinking. I want more of You and today I ask You to help me to take the limits off. I thank You and surrender my way to Your way that You may use me how You see fit. In Jesus' name, Amen!

<u>Journal question</u>

Name your "it." Have you been fooling yourself about the "it" that you have let go? Or has "it" crept back in? How do you keep giving "it" back over to the Lord?

_____

_____

_____

_____

_____

_____

_____

_____

_____

_____

_____

_____

_____

_____

Day 21: Bigger

In the silence I could feel and see His presence being wrapped around me. I was so small and He was so big. I serve a great God. He is **bigger** than anything that concerns me. He is **bigger** than my fears, my worries, my anxieties, my doubts, etc. I overcome all of that through the blood of my precious Savior Jesus Christ. There is safety in His presence. I am reminded of the scripture in **Psalm 16:11** that tells me that in His presence **there is fullness of joy and at His right hand are pleasures forevermore**. That is such a comfort. In the silence I press into His presence. In that place there is nothing in my life that is **bigger** than the One who loves me with an everlasting love.

Meditate on Scripture

> *You will show me the path of life;*
> *In Your presence is fullness of joy;*

At Your right hand are pleasures forevermore. (Psalm 16:11, NKJV)

The Lord has appeared of old to me, saying: "Yes, I have loved you with an everlasting love; Therefore with lovingkindness I have drawn you. (Jeremiah 13:3, NKJV)

Prayer

Hallelujah Lord You are great and greatly to be praised! Thank You for reminding me that You are greater than anything that comes against me, including my own thoughts and worries. I exalt You as Sovereign Lord over ALL. I praise You for the blood of Jesus that has brought complete freedom and victory in my life. Please remind me and do not let me forget just how great You are and how much BIGGER You are than anything that comes my way. I love and praise You in the matchless name of Jesus, Amen!

<u>Journal question</u>

What have you made bigger than God?

_____

_____

_____

_____

_____

_____

_____

_____

_____

_____

_____

_____

_____

_____

_____

_____

_____

_____

Exhortation as you End
(But Really Begin…)

Pray for wisdom and understanding. In the silence I ask God to flood my spirit so that I can understand what He is showing me. There is something that He is speaking, but it is only found in the deepest places. This cannot be something that is done only on occasion, but this is a want, a need, and a desire so strong that nothing will keep you from it. There are so many noisy voices and circumstances that would try to invade the silence. Guard the silence and hold it as precious; there is where you will hear what you must then speak out. I can't find Him with occasional prayers and Bible reading. I find Him in consistency. The more I give, the more I want. The more I seek, the more I find.

In Proverbs 18:21, the scripture tells us that life and death is in the power of the tongue. Use these daily declarations to speak into your own life. Write your own. Use the breath of God to speak life so that you can continually walk in the presence of God. Faith comes by hearing. Speak out loud! Use the words that you have in your mouth to draw near to your Heavenly Father who desires to meet you right where you are each day and in the Silence.

Daily Declarations

Lord, I confess that I am Your handiwork, made in Your image and after Your likeness. There is no one else like me. I am unique. I am fearfully and wonderfully made. I am marvelous in Your sight and the apple of Your eye. I am highly favored and blessed beyond measure and I declare that it is so in Jesus Name.

God, You are on the throne high and lifted up and You are MY Father! Your supply is all sufficient. You are not caught off guard, nor taken by surprise. God, You know the end from the beginning. Your love is unstoppable and more than my mind or heart can comprehend; but what I can comprehend is more than enough! I love You, Lord!

Lord, You are my light and my salvation so I will not fear. When I sit in darkness you are a light to me. Lord, I am the head and not the tail. I am the righteousness of God in Christ Jesus. I take authority over all the power of the enemy according to Your word. I rejoice that my name is written in heaven. Lord, I thank You that I am reconciled back to You and that I am made in Your image. I walk by faith. Thank you for counting it to me for righteousness and it is so in Jesus' name.

Lord, I declare that I walk in divine health and wholeness. I am the righteousness of God in Christ Jesus. I present my body as a living sacrifice holy and acceptable to God because that is my reasonable service. My body is the temple where the Holy Spirit dwells and He will not live in an unclean body. I have a sound mind and emotions. My will is submitted to God. I seek peace and pursue it. I walk in the peace of God that surpasses understanding and the joy of the Lord is my strength. I am whole and complete in Christ the Messiah and Anointed One. And it is so.

References

www.dictionary.com

www.biblegateway.com

21 Days of Silent Reflection with the Lord

JOURNAL

Silence Journal

_____

_____

_____

_____

_____

_____

_____

_____

_____

_____

_____

_____

_____

_____

_____

_____

_____

_____

Silence Journal

_____

_____

_____

_____

_____

_____

_____

_____

_____

_____

_____

_____

_____

_____

_____

_____

_____

_____

Silence Journal

_____

_____

_____

_____

_____

_____

_____

_____

_____

_____

_____

_____

_____

_____

_____

_____

_____

_____

_____

Silence Journal

_____

_____

_____

_____

_____

_____

_____

_____

_____

_____

_____

_____

_____

_____

_____

_____

_____

_____

Silence Journal

_____

_____

_____

_____

_____

_____

_____

_____

_____

_____

_____

_____

_____

_____

_____

_____

_____

_____

_____

Silence Journal

_____

_____

_____

_____

_____

_____

_____

_____

_____

_____

_____

_____

_____

_____

_____

_____

_____

_____

_____

_____

Silence Journal

_____

_____

_____

_____

_____

_____

_____

_____

_____

_____

_____

_____

_____

_____

_____

_____

_____

_____

Silence Journal

_____

_____

_____

_____

_____

_____

_____

_____

_____

_____

_____

_____

_____

_____

_____

_____

_____

_____

_____

Silence Journal

_____

_____

_____

_____

_____

_____

_____

_____

_____

_____

_____

_____

_____

_____

_____

_____

_____

_____

_____

Silence Journal

_____

_____

_____

_____

_____

_____

_____

_____

_____

_____

_____

_____

_____

_____

_____

_____

_____

_____

_____

Silence Journal

_____

_____

_____

_____

_____

_____

_____

_____

_____

_____

_____

_____

_____

_____

_____

_____

_____

_____

_____

Printed in the USA
CPSIA information can be obtained
at www.ICGtesting.com
LVHW010407161223
766567LV00004B/267

9 781942 871910